HISTORY OPENS WINDOWS

The SUMERIANS

JANE SHUTER

Heinemann Library
Chicago, Illinois

© 2002 Reed Educational & Professional Publishing
Published by Heinemann Library,
an imprint of Reed Educational & Professional Publishing,
Chicago, Illinois
Customer Service 888-454-2279
Visit our website at www.heinemannlibrary.com

Designed by Roslyn Broder
Printed in Hong Kong

06 05 04 03 02
10 9 8 7 6 5 4 3 2 1

Library of Congress Cataloging-in-Publication Data
Shuter, Jane.
   The Sumerians / Jane Shuter.
      p. cm. – (History opens windows)
Includes bibliographical references and index.
Summary: Presents an overview of the ancient Sumerian culture,
discussing government, recreation, trade, travel, family life, food,
occupations, and entertainment.
   ISBN 1-58810-592-X (lib. bdg.)   ISBN 1-4034-0027-X (pbk. bdg.)
   1. Sumerians—Juvenile literature. [1. Sumerians.] I. Title. II.
Series.
   DS72 .S56 2001
   935'.0049995—dc21
                                    2001004458

Acknowledgments
The author and publishers are grateful to the following for permission to reproduce copyright material: pp. 8, 25 Scala/Art Resource; pp. 9, 11, 19 Michael Holford; p. 10 Bridgeman Art Library, Iraq Museum, Baghdad; p. 12 Victor Boswell/National Geographic Society; pp. 13, 26 Gianni Dagli Orti/Corbis; p. 14 Georg Gerster/National Geographic Society; p. 16 Nik Wheeler/Corbis; p. 20 Courtesy of the Oriental Institute of the University of Chicago; p. 22 Peter Willi/SuperStock; pp. 23, 30 Erich Lessing/Art Resource; p. 24 Burstein Collection/Corbis; pp. 28, 29 British Museum/ Bridgeman Art Library

Illustrations: p. 4 Eileen Mueller Neill; pp. 7, 17, 18, 21, 27 David Westerfield
Cover photograph courtesy of Michael Holford

Every effort has been made to contact copyright holders of any material reproduced in this book. Any omissions will be rectified in subsequent printings if notice is given to the publisher.

Some words are shown in bold, **like this.** You can find out what they mean by looking in the glossary.

A note about dates: in this book, dates are followed by the letters B.C.E. (Before the Common Era) or C.E. (Common Era). This instead of using the older abbreviations B.C. and A.D. The date numbers are the same in both systems.

Contents

Introduction

This map shows Ancient Mesopotamia in
Sumerian times. The rivers and coastline were
a different shape than the shape they are now.

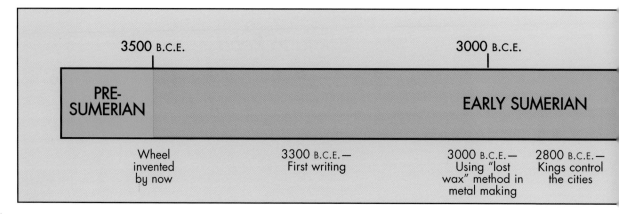

3500 B.C.E.		3000 B.C.E.	
PRE-SUMERIAN			**EARLY SUMERIAN**
Wheel invented by now	3300 B.C.E.— First writing	3000 B.C.E.— Using "lost wax" method in metal making	2800 B.C.E.— Kings control the cities

People first lived in Mesopotamia more then 9,000 years ago. "Mesopotamia" means "the land between the rivers." Sumer was between the Tigris and Euphrates Rivers, to the south, where the rivers often flooded. The flooding left a rich mud that crops could grow in. The Sumerians used the rivers and dug **irrigation canals** to water their crops and to travel by boat.

The Sumerian period started in about 3500 B.C.E., when people began to live in cities, each with its own king. In about 2330 B.C.E., Akkadians from the north took over Sumer and ruled until about 2280 B.C.E. Then Sumerian kings took over again. In about 2200 B.C.E. the kings of Ur built an **empire,** which broke up into separate cities after about 150 years. In 2004 B.C.E. Ur was captured. This is seen as the end of the Sumerian period, although later rulers still called themselves "king of Sumer and Akkad."

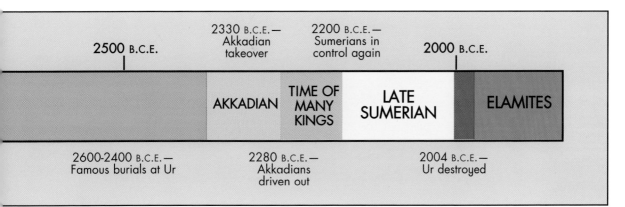

City-States

The Sumerians did not have a single ruler. Instead, each city and the lands around it were ruled by a different king. This was called a **city-state.** Some city-states were bigger and more powerful than others. Sometimes they fought with each other and sometimes they traded with each other. Children of different kings would marry each other, to keep the peace between their city-states. The Akkadians, who lived north of Sumer, also had city-states.

We see the Sumerians as a single group, even though they had many rulers. This is because all Sumerians had the same religion, organized themselves in the same way, and used the same written and spoken language. Other groups living in Mesopotamia at the same time, like the Akkadians who took over Sumer for a while, saw themselves as different groups.

*This modern drawing of the city of Ur is based on what **archaeologists** have discovered.*

The *ziggurat* and other important buildings were in the middle of the city.

Ordinary people lived and worked around the edge of the city.

The city also had mud brick walls for safety.

The river was made to flow around the city, to keep it safe.

How Sumer Was Ruled

Early Sumerian cities were run by groups of male citizens. They could choose a "great man," called a *patesi,* to rule in times of war or crisis. Over time, these men became more and more important. By 2800 B.C.E. each Sumerian **city-state** was ruled by a king, who chose the next ruler. Later, Sumerian kings ruled in families and said they were given the job by the god of the city.

Historians think this bronze head of a king is Sargon, sometimes called Naram-Sin.

This stone carving shows Ur Nanshe, ruler of Lagash in about 2480 B.C.E., carrying a basket of bricks on his head. He is acting out his job as "builder of the city" in a religious **ceremony.**

Each city-state "belonged" to a different god. The city of Ur served Nannu, the moon god, while the city of Uruk served Inanna, the goddess of love and war. Each city had a large walled area in the middle where the **temples** were. The biggest temple was for the city's god. These walled areas also held storehouses and government buildings. The king ran the city-state for its god. His job was to keep the people well fed, the temples in good condition, and the city safe from outsiders.

9

War

War was a part of Sumerian life. The **city-states** often fought each other. They also fought invaders from nearby countries who tried to take over. Each Sumerian city-state had its own army. The armies were not very big at first, but they were well-trained and had good weapons. The soldiers had metal-tipped spears, daggers, large shields, and leather armor. Sumerians are the first people we know of who used **tactics** such as attacking in a block marching in step.

This king's helmet made from silver and gold was too valuable to use in battle. But when they fought, kings wore metal helmets, not leather ones like their soldiers.

10

In this picture of an army going into battle, you can see the soldiers' armor and the chariots they used.

The Sumerians were the first people that we know used wheels. They used them to build carts and war **chariots.** The chariots were useful for carrying weapons and shields as the army marched to war. They were also used for fighting. One man drove the chariot, while another stood behind the driver and threw spears at the enemy. Soldiers also used battle axes with long handles to fight from chariots. Daggers were used in hand-to-hand fighting.

Religion

The Sumerians believed in many different gods and goddesses who controlled the weather, the flooding of the rivers, and almost all parts of everyday life. They worshiped these gods and goddesses at public **temples,** but also at smaller **shrines** in their own homes. Priests were very important because they were the link between the gods and the people. Religious **festivals** were held several times a month and on special days, like the celebration of the New Year.

These statues were left as offerings at Sumerian temples. The ones with big eyes are thought to be gods.

Each Sumerian **city-state** was protected by one of the gods, and people prayed mainly to that god. However, they did not want the other gods to get jealous and harm the city, so they prayed to them, too. Each Sumerian also had a god as his or her own protector. They prayed to the god of the city about things that affected the city, such as a good **harvest.** If they were sick they prayed to their own god or goddess. The Sumerians believed in a life after death and buried their dead with things they would need in the afterlife, such as clothes, furniture, and food.

The peoples who followed the Sumerians had many of the same gods and goddesses. Here is a Babylonian ruler, standing in front of the sun god.

Temples

Temples were an important part of Sumerian religion. They were built by workers and **slaves** from mud bricks on a mud brick platform. By 2000 B.C.E. these temples had become **ziggurats.** Ziggurats have three platforms, one on top of the other, each smaller than the one below. At the top of the temple was a **shrine** where the god or goddess lived. Priests visited the shrines every day to pray and leave offerings. Priestesses and musicians also worked in the temples.

Sumerian temples were very rich and owned a lot of land outside the city. Some priests ran the religious activities of the temples. Others ran the day-to-day activities, such as listing all the crops grown.

This is a reconstruction of a ziggurat. The only entrance to a ziggurat was by the steep staircase in the center.

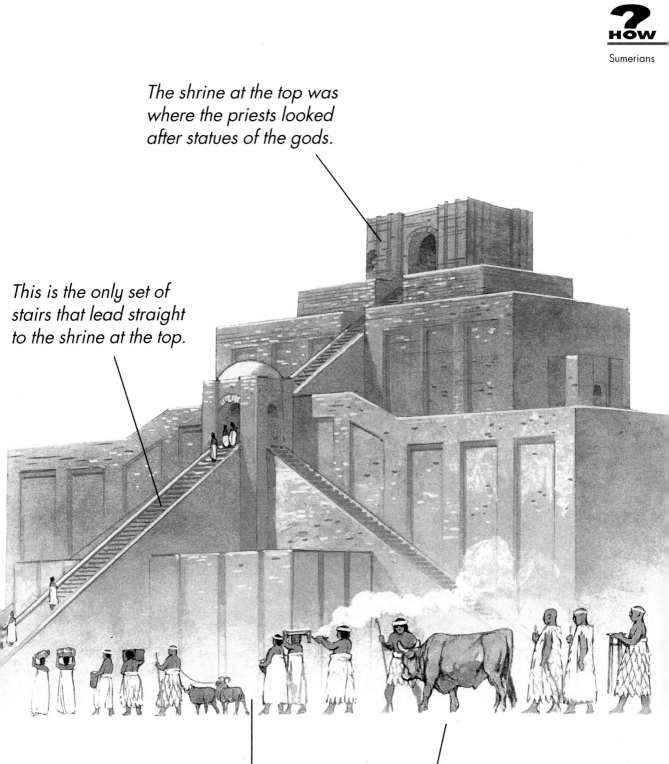

The shrine at the top was where the priests looked after statues of the gods.

This is the only set of stairs that lead straight to the shrine at the top.

The bottom layer of the ziggurat measured 205 feet (62 meters) by 141 feet (43 meters) and was 36 feet (11 meters) high.

Animals and other things were brought as sacrifices on special days.

Travel and Trade

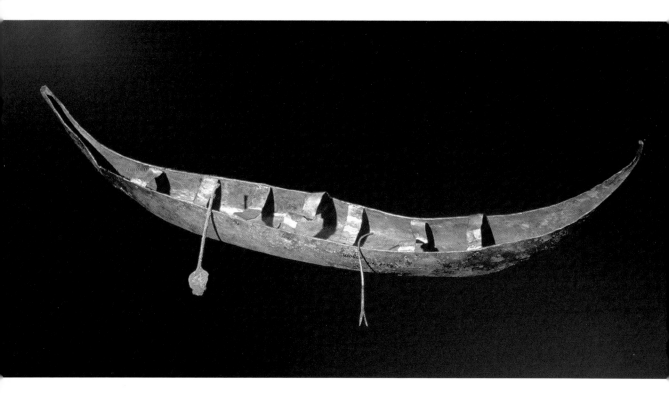

Ordinary Sumerians did not travel far from their **city-states.** It could be dangerous, because other city-states were not always friendly. But they did travel locally in several ways. Most people walked or rode donkeys. Donkeys were also used to carry heavy loads. The Sumerians used wheels, so they could also carry goods in carts. The system of rivers and **canals** in Mesopotamia meant that people could also travel by boat. Boats were especially useful for moving heavy things, such as loads of mud bricks, from place to place.

This beautiful silver model shows a Sumerian boat. These boats were used to travel along the canals and rivers.

Sumerian traders traveled in order to trade grain and cloth for goods such as gold, shells, decorative stones, and **bitumen** to use as mortar in buildings. Sumer was in a good place in the trade route system. Many of the goods the traders bought came from far away. But they often only had to go to the nearest big trading town to buy these things. If they did travel further, they could buy things more cheaply and make more money.

This map shows the most important trade routes for Sumerian merchants and the most important goods they wanted to buy.

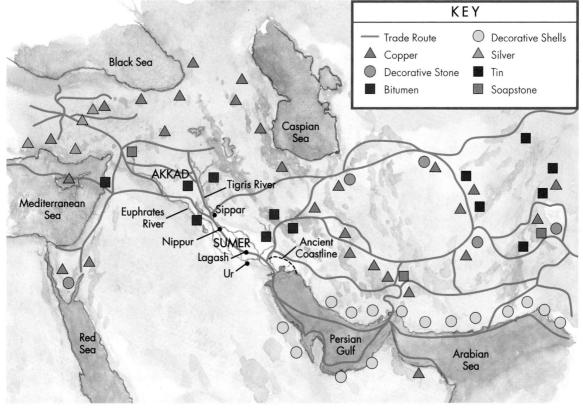

KEY

- —— Trade Route
- ▲ Copper
- ⬤ Decorative Stone
- ◼ Bitumen
- ◯ Decorative Shells
- ▲ Silver
- ◼ Tin
- ◼ Soapstone

Farming and Food

Farming was very important to the Sumerians. Each **city-state** had to grow enough food to feed its people. Most city-states tried to grow more grain than they needed. Then they could use the extra grain to trade for things they needed from other places.

Sumerian farmers used ponds and **canals** to control the water of the two rivers. They used several kinds of plows, as well as simple wooden tools. Grain was the most important crop. It could be made into flour, bread, beer, and porridge. There were special religious **ceremonies** for planting grain, but not for other crops.

The Sumerians invented a seed sowing machine, which could plant seeds more quickly and evenly than sowing by hand.

Sumerian farmers kept cattle, sheep, and goats.

Sumerian farmers also grew other crops, including beans, onions, garlic, lettuce, cucumbers, leeks, turnips, and mustard. Many plants were used by doctors to make **ointments** for treating illnesses. They also made **poultices** to stop infection by mixing plants and herbs, warming them, and then putting them on cuts.

Farmers kept cattle for milk, meat, and for use as work animals. Sheep and goats were kept for milk, meat, and wool. Donkeys were used to carry heavy loads. Animal skins were turned into leather, used mainly for armor.

19

Houses

Many Sumerians lived in one-roomed houses made from mud brick. They had **reed** roofs and a **hearth** at one end for cooking. Homes were usually whitewashed inside and out. In these homes, people slept on a raised mud brick sleeping platform and had very little furniture. Richer people had several rooms around a courtyard and sometimes even a second floor. In some cities there may have been a few three-story buildings. These would have been shared by several families.

People usually cooked over an open fire. They could cook their food in clay pots that sat in the flames, or they could roast it over the fire. Most people did not eat meat every day. They ate vegetables, cheese, and bread, and drank beer and milk.

Sumerians who lived outside the city often lived in one-roomed reed huts, like the one shown here.

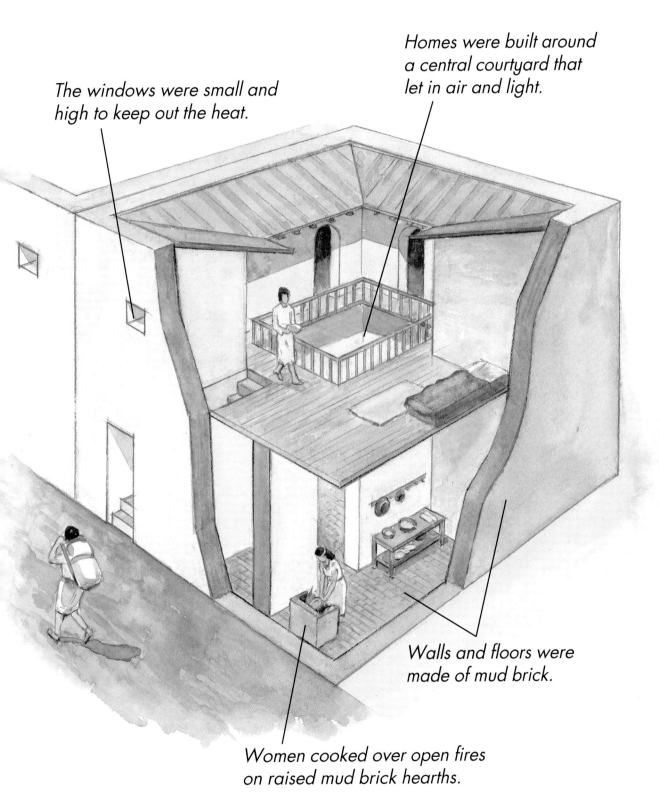

The windows were small and high to keep out the heat.

Homes were built around a central courtyard that let in air and light.

Walls and floors were made of mud brick.

Women cooked over open fires on raised mud brick hearths.

Families

In Sumer, parents arranged their children's marriages. Men worked and made the family decisions. Women took care of the home and raised the children. Some women did run businesses. These were usually widows who took over the family business when their husbands died. But girls did not go to school. They were taught to run a home by their mothers.

Some boys learned to read and write so they could become **scribes.** Scribes were important in the government of a **city-state.** It took years to learn the symbols, words, and phrases of Sumerian writing by heart. The boys also studied math, geography, and astronomy.

This statue may show a teacher. Teachers were important people in Sumer. You can tell that this man is important by the clothes he is wearing. Teachers were always men.

Going to school cost money, so only boys from wealthy families could go. The rest learned how to do their fathers' jobs. There were many different jobs available in the cities. Some potters, metalworkers, jewelers, and other craft workers worked for themselves. Others worked for the **temples,** the king, or wealthy families. In the countryside, boys grew up to be farmers or fishermen.

Wealthy families might have **slaves** working for them. Slaves were usually prisoners who had been captured in war, but some crimes had slavery as a punishment. Slaves could be freed at any time.

Boys learning to be jewelers had a lot to learn before they could produce something as beautiful as this. They began with very simple necklaces and headdresses.

Clothes

Sumerian clothes were made from finely woven linen and wool. The thread was looped and bunched. In carvings from the time, it looks like tufts of sheepskin and fleece or just fleece. Working people wore simple clothes that were easy to move and work in. Rich, important people wore longer clothes, made from more expensive cloth. They wore leather shoes instead of **reed** sandals.

Rich and important women wore beautiful and expensive jewelry. This jewelry was found in Ur, in a queen's grave.

Early Sumerian men wore skirts that reached from the waist to the knee. They shaved their heads and faces. Women wore layered skirts and covered their heads and upper bodies with shawls. They put their long hair up in complicated hairstyles.

Later, the styles changed. Men wore a **tunic** or a longer skirt. Some of them grew beards and long hair. Women wore straight skirts or long tunics.

This statue of a woman shows the complicated loops of thread used to make clothes. The woman is wearing a skirt and shawl. Her feet are bare.

25

Writing and Calendars

The Sumerians were the first people to develop a written language. At first, they used pictures. The first use of these was on small carved seals that were used to make marks in soft clay.

In about 3300 B.C.E. the Sumerians began using symbols instead of pictures. These symbols were pressed into flat pieces of clay with a wedge-shaped **stylus.** This type of writing was called cuneiform. Early writing was mostly for record-keeping, but by 2800 B.C.E. the Sumerians had begun writing down stories, prayers, history, and songs as well.

This clay tablet is covered with cuneiform symbols. They are a list of sheep and goats traded from one person to another.

The Sumerians needed calendars to keep track of when the rivers would flood, when to plant and **harvest** crops, and when special **festivals** for the gods should be held. They had two seasons, summer and winter. They divided the year up into 12 months of 29 or 30 days. All **city-states** used the same system, but some of them used different names for the months.

The Sumerians divided the day into two twelve hour blocks, like we do, but their days ran from one sunset to the next. They told time by using pots with the hours marked on them. The pots were filled with water that dripped slowly away through a hole in the side. The level of the water told you what time it was.

The diagram below shows how Sumerian writing changed from pictures to symbols.

PICTOGRAM MEANING	3500 B.C.E.	2500 B.C.E.	1800 B.C.E.	900 B.C.E.	700 B.C.E.
HEAD					
STREAM					
DRINK					

Free Time

Music, singing, and dancing were all important to the Sumerians, both for everyday life and for religious **ceremonies.** They had several kinds of musical instruments, including harps, lyres, drums, pipes, and tambourines. Some people were trained as musicians, but many ordinary people could play an instrument.

The Sumerians also played board games. The most famous board game of all was found in the Royal Tombs of Ur. **Archaeologists** have found a written description of the game and have discovered how it may have been played.

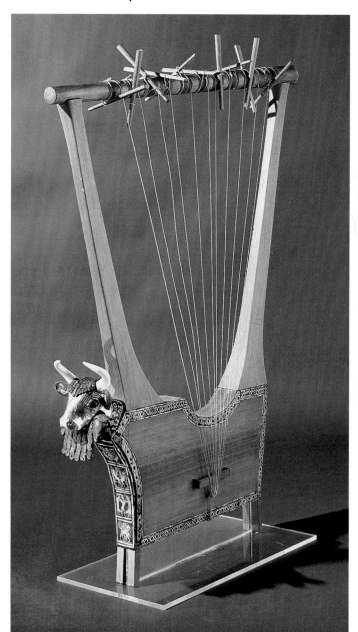

This beautiful lyre would have been used in the home of a king or a very rich man.

The Royal Game of Ur was found in a grave from about 2600 B.C.E.

The different patterns on the squares meant different things. Some squares were lucky, and they gave help to a player who landed on them. Others were unlucky.

Both players shared the center strip. When counters were here they could be taken by the other player.

The winner was the player who got all their counters to this square first.

The game was a race game. The players started here and followed the red and blue dotted lines.

These counters were used to race around the board.

End of Empire

In 2200 B.C.E. Sumer had been strong under one king, who ruled from Ur. By 2020 B.C.E. the Sumerian **empire** had broken up into **city-states** again. At first these city-states were still ruled by Sumerian kings. But in 2004 B.C.F. Ur was invaded, captured, and looted by Elamites from the east. Sumer became a land of city-states that were ruled by different peoples. This is usually seen as the end of the Sumerian period. It was not until 1792 B.C.E. that this part of Mesopotamia was united again, this time under the Babylonian leader Hammurabi.

The Elamites did not rule Sumer for long. They were driven out by the Amorites. This carving shows the taking of the city.

Glossary

archaeologist   person who studies people and objects from the past

bitumen   tar-like material used to stick things together

canal   deep ditch filled with water that is used for boats or for irrigation

ceremony   set of acts with religious meaning

chariot   small, horse-drawn vehicle

city-state   a city and the towns, villages, and land around it that are controlled by the ruler of the city

empire   group of territories or lands controlled by one country

festival   time of celebration with special events and entertainment

harvest   season when crops are gathered; or, to gather a crop

hearth   area in front of a fireplace

irrigation   bringing water to crops by using canals or other methods

ointment   greasy medicine that is used on the skin

poultice   medicine and herbs that are heated and placed on the body

reed   tall, thick grass that grows in wet areas

scribe   person whose job is to read, write, and keep records

shrine   special place for worshipping gods or dead relatives

slave   someone who belongs to someone else and is forced to work without pay

stylus   pointed instrument used for writing on clay tablets

tactic   a planned action for some purpose

temple   building for religious worship

tunic   knee-length belted garment

ziggurat   pyramid-shaped temple made of layers, each smaller than the one below

More Books to Read

An older reader can help you with these books:

Landau, Elaine. *The Sumerians.* Brookfield, Conn.: Millbrook Press, Inc., 1997.

Oakes, Lorna. *Assyria & Mesopotamia.* New York: Anness Publishing, Inc., 2001.

Index